Th(
SOUTH ...

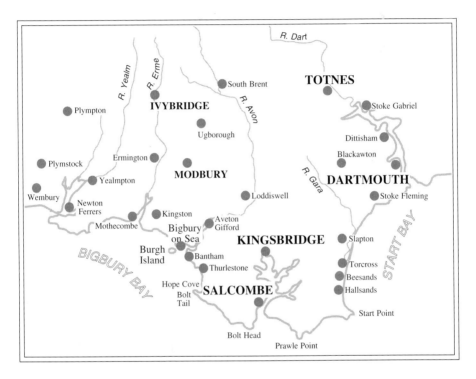

South Brent

TOTNES

Stoke Gabriel

Plympton

IVYBRIDGE

R. Yealm

R. Erme

R. Avon

R. Dart

Ugborough

Dittisham

Blackawton

Ermington

Plymstock

Yealmpton

MODBURY

DARTMOUTH

R. Gara

Loddiswell

Stoke Fleming

Wembury

Newton
Ferrers

Kingston

Aveton
Gifford

Mothecombe

Bigbury
on Sea

KINGSBRIDGE

Slapton

START BAY

Burgh
Island

Bantham

BIGBURY BAY

Thurlestone

Torcross

Beesands

Hope Cove

Bolt
Tail

SALCOMBE

Hallsands

Start Point

Bolt Head

Prawle Point

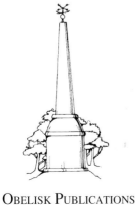

Chips Barber
with Sally Barber

OBELISK PUBLICATIONS

Also Available by the author:
Around & About the Haldon Hills
The Lost City of Exeter
Diary of a Dartmoor Walker
Diary of a Devonshire Walker
The Great Little Dartmoor Book
The Great Little Exeter Book
Made in Devon (with David FitzGerald)
Dartmoor in Colour / Plymouth in Colour
Burgh Island and Bigbury Bay (with Judy Chard)
Dark & Dastardly Dartmoor (with Sally Barber)
Exeter in Colour / Torbay in Colour
Ghosts of Exeter (with Sally Barber)
The Great Little Totnes Book (with Bill Bennett)
Tales of the Teign (with Judy Chard)
Ten Family Walks on Dartmoor (with Sally Barber)
The Great Little Plymouth Book
Weird & Wonderful Dartmoor (with Sally Barber)
Ghastly and Ghostly Devon (with Sally Barber)
Dawlish and Dawlish Warren
Also Available about this area:
Under Sail through South Devon and Dartmoor, Raymond B. Cattell
Tales of the Unexplained in Devon, Judy Chard
The Totnes Collection, Bill Bennett
Boat Trip Down the Dart, Bob Mann
Walks in the South Hams, Brian Carter

For further details of these or any of our titles, please contact
Obelisk Publications at the address below or telephone Exeter (0392) 68556.

Acknowledgements
All photographs by or belonging to Chips Barber
All maps by Sally Barber
Special thanks to WJ Reynolds for his help and advice

First published in 1992 by
Obelisk Publications, 2 Church Hill, Pinhoe, Exeter, Devon
Designed by Chips and Sally Barber,
Typeset by Sally Barber
Printed in Great Britain by
Sprint Print, Okehampton Place, Exeter

The South Hams

There was once a brochure which proudly stated that "The South Hams **is** South Devon" but, although I agree with the sentiment, geographically and administratively that is not quite true. However it can be claimed that The South Hams is the most beautiful part of South Devon, even the most beautiful part of all England. I would not gain say that.

For this little book, 'The South Hams' is the area which is bounded by the River Dart on the eastern margin, the ever-busy A38 along the northern limit, the River Yealm on the tapering western boundary, and the southern side by that spectacular coastline which goes on mile after mile. This is an area which is a bit bigger than the Isle of Wight, even remarkably similar in shape, but there the resemblance ends!

In such a small volume as this, covering such an extensive area, I must be more concise than I would have liked when featuring some of the places, particularly the Bigbury Bay area to which I have already devoted an entire book, *Burgh Island and Bigbury Bay*. Also it is my policy not to duplicate too many stories, so I have tried to give greater coverage to people and places not already covered in other titles.

We will start at Totnes, go down the Dart and then follow the coastline around to the Yealm. This will take us past some wonderful places including Dartmouth, Torcross, Beesands, Hallsands, Start, Prawle, Salcombe, Bolt Head and Tail, Hope, Thurlestone, Bigbury and Burgh Island, Mothecombe, Newton and Noss. We will follow the other main rivers of the South Hams – the many fingered estuary up to Kingsbridge, the Avon up to South Brent and the Erme up to Dartmoor's edge at Ivybridge. On the way we will visit some of those other places where time stands still, where the grave stones in the churchyards reveal that people in this healthy environment lived very long lives. There is much to see and much to do and it would take one of those very long life times to cover it all!

Totnes has been nicknamed 'The Gateway to the South Hams'; although this presupposes that you approach the area from the north east, it is nevertheless an appropriate term. Most guide books will include a picture of the (reconstructed) East Gate arch which straddles the main street, and/or include a picture of the old Totnes Bridge spanning the Dart. *The Great Little Totnes Book* is no exception, covering these and much more!

Totnes is one of Devon's four ancient and original boroughs, yet in terms of population is well down the rank order. Fortunately there is no correlation between quantity and quality, quite the reverse.

It is now traditional for Totnesian traders to 'tog up' on Tuesdays in Elizabethan clothes. This has turned what was the quietest trading day into by far the busiest, has enabled charities to earn many thousands of pounds and has caught the media's attention. It is appropriate for Totnes to have an 'Elizabethan day' as the

town prospered greatly in that particular era before, apparently, stagnating and allowing other towns of lesser note to develop faster. Perhaps that is no bad thing as the legacy of languishing behind in the industrial rat race is a series of wonderful buildings, butterwalks, piazzas and an impressive waterfront. So get ye to Totnes on a Tuesday and savour ye olde atmosphere but get ye verily there early as ye olde traffic queues can tail back almost to the edge of Paignton on dull days!

Every year thousands of people treat themselves to a river cruise down the Dart from Totnes to Dartmouth. The journey takes about one and a quarter hours and is packed with places and views to savour. There is so much history to discover that I recommend you read *Boat Trip Down the Dart* by Bob Mann. He gives a much fuller coverage than I am able to, to this important river that Queen Victoria dubbed 'The English Rhine'.

Here then is but a potted account of what you might hear or see on the ten miles of Dart between 'the Good Town of Totnes' and Dartmouth, 'the Town for all

Seasons' – although the ferries only run in the summer season!

Although theory suggests a calm and sheltered passage on this mainly north–south journey, the vicissitudes of the weather and funnelling nature of the many valleys often combine to create windy conditions on the water.

The first major house high on the hill above the west bank is Sharpham, built in 1770 by Captain Philemon Pownell RN. He was given a substantial reward for capturing a Spanish vessel but the poor chap never got to live in his mansion. The house was finished more than half a century after it was started and has had some distinguished residents, including the Bastards and the Durants. The latter gave their name to the pub at Ashprington, a picturesque hilltop village about half a mile from Sharpham.

The Dart snakes in a big loop around the Sharpham Estate before it is joined, from the west, by Bow Creek. This tributary is fed by two rivers, the Wash and the Harbourne. This is countryside best explored on foot or, if your nerves can stand it, by car. The popularity of villages like Cornworthy, Tuckenhay and Ashprington has grown visibly in recent years and the narrow, twisty lanes are of the 'slam on the brakes' variety. It is possible that a certain TV chef may have contributed to this, having bought a pub at Tuckenhay.

Those whose interest lies in industrial archaeology will be able to see the old paper mill, now converted for leisure purposes, further up the inlet near Tuckenhay Bridge. The immediate reaction, on seeing it, is that it is disproportionately large for the location it is in, more like a Yorkshire mill. It began life in 1829 and produced high quality hand made papers. These were used, for many years, in making English bank notes.

What is older than Methuselah, has a trunk bigger than the biggest elephant's (waistline) and has spent all of its incredibly long life at church? The answer is the amazing yew tree at Stoke Gabriel church, so amazing that it invariably merits a mention in every guide book that covers this village.

Stoke Gabriel is an attractive, sprawling village which is a popular spot on fine days, with its mill pool and attractive waterfront, for the many thousands of visitors to nearby Torbay. On the journey down the river the village is not as conspicuous as many would believe as it shyly turns its face towards its own creek.

The next large house, down river, on the same bank is Sandridge Park, site of

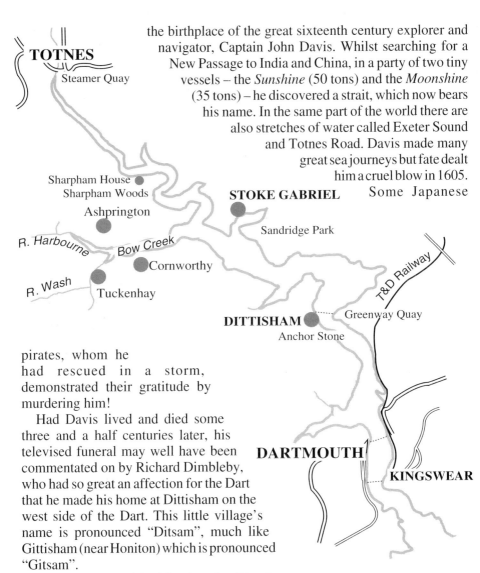

the birthplace of the great sixteenth century explorer and navigator, Captain John Davis. Whilst searching for a New Passage to India and China, in a party of two tiny vessels – the *Sunshine* (50 tons) and the *Moonshine* (35 tons) – he discovered a strait, which now bears his name. In the same part of the world there are also stretches of water called Exeter Sound and Totnes Road. Davis made many great sea journeys but fate dealt him a cruel blow in 1605. Some Japanese pirates, whom he had rescued in a storm, demonstrated their gratitude by murdering him!

Had Davis lived and died some three and a half centuries later, his televised funeral may well have been commentated on by Richard Dimbleby, who had so great an affection for the Dart that he made his home at Dittisham on the west side of the Dart. This little village's name is pronounced "Ditsam", much like Gittisham (near Honiton) which is pronounced "Gitsam".

Dittisham was visited by Anneka Rice in a Channel Four *Treasure Hunt* series. She visited the Ferry Boat Inn but had a little difficulty in locating the bell hanging behind the bar – so much excitement for so little a village!

Previously the most exciting adventure occurred at 'Ditsam Regatta' when the champion boat *Black Plum* was challenged by a sleek and smart vessel called *The Veronica*. The race, over two miles, was a close contest but *The Veronica* edged clear and an upset was on the cards. However the wily skipper of *Black Plum*, Sammy Coombes, moved over into the strong ebb flow current and shot past *The*

Veronica to record a famous victory. The winning vessel was well named as Dittisham is famous for its variety of plums which will only, so it is said, grow in this location in this country. They are delicious and are believed to have been introduced from Germany by a local man in about 1869.

It is an odd statistic that some 18,000 people have been buried in the graveyard of St George's Church at Dittisham. Odd because the village has a population of a mere 500 or so.

Death was not very far away from the mind of our next character and there is precious little mystery as to her identity – Agatha Christie. She chose Greenway House as one of her homes and contrived to write many of her cunningly crafted books here.

Greenway was the birthplace of the Elizabethan Sir Humphrey Gilbert, who was half-brother to Sir Walter Raleigh. His record of achievement was quite considerable as he was given a brief to take possession and inhabit unknown or remote lands which had not yet been previously claimed by any Christian prince. He made a settlement in Newfoundland and established the fishing trade there. Alas doom and gloom followed. The story goes that whilst sailing eastward from Campobellow, his entire crew witnessed the ghostly apparition of a giant lion gliding across the water. As it passed them it gave out a great roar. Almost instantly a violent storm erupted and Sir Humphrey, with bible in hand, went down with his vessel *The Squirrel*. The accompanying ship, the *Golden Hind*, survived and made it back to England.

The Anchor Stone is a curious rocky obstacle in the river just below Dittisham. As various small craft have been wont to wash onto it, a marker exists to warn other river users. Its alternative name was 'The Scold's Stone' and in the days when men treated their wives in a way that could lead to prosecution today, this stone was used as a place to maroon, deliberately, those who had nagged their menfolk too much.

However, a more acceptable mental image of the stone can be conjured up of a contented Sir Walter Raleigh prostrate upon it, engaged in puffing away at his silver pipe. He is charged with introducing tobacco to this country and he would probably turn in his grave if he knew the scale of what he had ignited! The notion of him smoking in quiet repose on the Anchor Stone may stem from a story that the first time he smoked tobacco was at Greenway. His servant, on entering the room, thought he was on fire and duly doused him with a bucket of water!

Raleigh made 'a packet' out of tobacco on a wager with Queen Elizabeth I. He bet that he could calculate the weight of the smoke, an idea which she was pleased to bet against. Raleigh weighed some tobacco, put it in his pipe, smoked it – and then weighed the ashes. The difference in weight must have 'gone up in smoke'. The Queen paid up.

It has also been claimed that the first potatoes grown in English soil were cultivated at Greenway.

The Dart narrows towards Dartmouth with the wooded hills towering above the river. Many television programmes have been made in this area and if you acquire my book *Made in Devon* you can read how the woods have played the part of the Amazon Rain Forest, whilst Kingswear has played the part of Exeter. Dartmouth has had so many roles that it is a star performer.

At Noss many fine vessels have been built, including Chay Blythe's *British Steel*. The shipyard of Philip and Sons was once the biggest local employer. Founded in 1858 it built a variety of craft from river steamers to light-ships (not in weight!). Today it concentrates on repair and maintenance work.

I like to think of the Dart as a moat protecting the glorious South Hams from the dense population of Torbay which lies not far away to the east. Climb any high hill to the west of the Dart and you will see the urban sprawl of Torbay poised ready to spread ever nearer this sacred kingdom. It has long been a necessity for people in this area to find the means to cross the river rather than go up or down it. The ferries, or floating bridges, cross this 'moat' at various points. No doubt some

clever statistician could come up with a meaningful figure of the cumulated time spent by all the car passengers waiting to cross the river. The statistic would no doubt then be harnessed to some poor individual and reveal that he or she spends an entire lifetime waiting to cross the river. If you ever find yourself in a queue at peak time on a Summer Bank Holiday, you will begin to suspect that the individual is yourself!

The actress Twiggy made a TV commercial, for a moped, on the Lower Ferry, and greatly endeared herself to those working it at the time. She had to cross many times before the filming was complete, but at least she didn't have to wait in a queue like the rest of us!

Dartmouth is a good example of how, in the main, the larger settlement has grown on the more sheltered west bank of an estuary. The hills which have limited its development rise steeply above the town. Extra land has been reclaimed by draining a creek and by other deviously clever methods. Unlike many Devonshire rivers, the Dart is deep in its lower reaches. Nature has created a haven for ships and there have been some famous comings and goings. *The Mayflower* spent a week undergoing repairs in the summer of 1620. Geoffrey Chaucer, author of the celebrated *Canterbury Tales,* made a pilgrimage to the town in 1373 and may well

have observed some of the people which became such colourful characters in his various chronicles.

Less peaceful were the various raiders intent on removing Dartmouth from the landscape. Amongst these the French have made various attempts but the town has survived all onslaughts. Today it is the invading tourist who comes borne on the breeze of river cruisers, in full steam care of the Torbay and Dartmouth railway, in comfort by coach, or under their own steam by car. The latter are not always lucky enough to secure a parking place, so a park and ride scheme exists to mop up the overflow. Along the waterfront the various river cruise companies tout for business.

The town is a network of narrow streets, full of unusual buildings. The most photographed, the Butterwalk, survived a Second World War bomb blast on Saturday, 13 February 1943 when it was rendered completely windowless and its eleven pillars were buckled to the extent that the building looked like a punch drunk boxer on the verge of keeling over for a knock out. However it was saved and is solid enough now. In the season it is decorated with flower tubs.

Famous inventor Thomas Newcomen was born at Dartmouth in 1663. His pumping engine, which drew water deep from the bottoms of mines, was of far reaching significance for the Industrial Revolution. A preserved atmospheric engine was installed, on the tercentenary of his birth, at the Royal Avenue Gardens and it is one of the oldest in existence having worked at Griff Colliery and latterly on the Coventry Canal until 1913.

The most dominant building in this landscape is The Britannia Royal Naval College which has sat facing the morning sunshine since 1905. It was here in April 1939 that the Queen met Prince Philip for the first time. The college has its roots in 1863 when the Admiralty moved the training ship HMS *Britannia* from

9

Portland to its moorings on the Dart. Subsequently it was joined by another old hulk, HMS *Hindustan*. The arrival of so many people to the district gave a boost to local trade and the presence of the college has been a boon to the town's economic prosperity.

Those who remember Dartmouth as it was years ago, will recall, with affection, a famous and brave vessel called *The Mew*. She was built in 1905 by William Downing Cox for the Great Western Railway. Her colours were of the GWR livery and she plied between Kingswear Station and 'Dartmouth Station'. The latter was a building built in the style and custom of a typical railway station, complete with booking office and other trimmings, but missing just one thing – a railway. People would purchase their tickets here, board *The Mew* (a Devonshire word for seagull) and head to Kingswear for their awaiting locomotive.

The Mew was a brave little boat for she went to Dunkirk and returned safely. On another occasion, in terrible weather conditions, a French destroyer *The Mistral* entered the Dart. A combination of swirling winds and tides caused her to drift helplessly towards the rocks between Bayard's Cove and Warfleet. Just as disaster seemed inevitable *The Mew*, firing on all cylinders, headed straight across the water. At the same time a French tug joined in and after much pushing, a great deal of arm waving and amidst great excitement, *The Mistral* was rescued.

Bayard's Cove is an attractive collection of buildings. It was a backcloth for the BBC's *The Onedin Line*, playing the part of Liverpool, a role it shared with Exeter (see *Made in Devon* for full details).

Downstream there are a pair of stone castles, Dartmouth and Kingswear. They were once linked by a most impressive chain, known as 'Jawbones', which kept out unwanted or enemy shipping.

From Dartmouth most people will find their way into the heart of the South Hams via the A379 coast road which follows the coast through Stoke Fleming and Strete, and on to Torcross, before veering inland to Kingsbridge. In the storms of early 1990 this road collapsed above Blackpool Sands. The resultant subsidence caused endless inconvenience for the local residents; traders lost their passing trade and great financial hardship was endured by pubs and shops.

Stoke Fleming is a rambling village situated very close to the sea, but still some 300 feet above sea level. Despite its elevated situation a proportion of its dwellings nestle into slopes which afford some protection from the prevailing south westerly wind. At the time of the Domesday Book it was much larger, and more important than Dartmouth, with a population of 250 – some five times that of Dartmouth (Townstal).

The village has grown steadily in population rising in every census, from 578 in 1801 to 989 in the 1981 figures. Needless to say none of the original inhabitants feature in both counts, although it is true that this particular area is highly conducive to longevity. A survey of those found buried in the churchyard will reveal that most of them were 'ancient' when they breathed their last.

Stoke Fleming is one of a minority of villages to grow in size. In the main, the settlements of the South Hams which are away from the major centres of population, however modest in size, have shown a general decline in population. Many of the smaller villages and hamlets have lost their schools, which have now been given over to fieldwork centres or have been converted into houses.

In the days before sophisticated navigational aids for mariners, the church of St Peter at Stoke Fleming was used as a marker by ships entering the mouth of the Dart. It has had a few notable rectors, including Elias Newcomen, who was the great grandfather of the inventor, Thomas Newcomen, and of course there was the amazing Richard Reynolds. He was well over eighty when he was turned out of his church in the Civil War (1642–46). However at the Restoration in 1660, he returned to die there at the age of about one hundred years old.

Further evidence of longevity was the lady who was over ninety when she died in 1937. Her father, George Parker Bidder, had been born in the year before Trafalgar (1805) and has a place in history as a genius, gifted with superb calculating skills, one of the cleverest persons who has ever lived! He too was buried at Stoke Fleming. In his lifetime he worked closely with his great friend, George Stephenson (of 'The Rocket' fame) to engineer railroads in Britain and across Europe. He constructed London's Victoria Docks and the concept of the swing bridge can be attributed to his mental agility. Despite these achievements he is best remembered for his arithmetical skills. His father made money by exhibiting George's impressive powers of multiplying or adding long columns of figures at little more than a glance. In Parliamentary committees he was particularly useful as he could spot a flaw in any calculation and it was not unusual for those with a vested interest to ask him not to remain in the room! From the high life of fame and glory, George now rests peacefully beneath South Hams skies.

From Stoke Fleming the A379 coast road, when it is intact, wends its way on towards Strete. Before it reaches there it plunges down to Blackpool Sands, a place which could not be a greater contrast to its famous Lancastrian namesake. Although everything in life is a matter of personal preference, I think this Blackpool in South Devon is much more beautiful.

However in 1404 it was the scene of a confrontation between two armies, the English and the French Bretons. Having already burnt down half of Plymouth, as revenge for English attacks on Breton ports, Dartmouth became the next target. Led by Du Chatel, the Bretons landed a few miles down the coast at Slapton and started marching towards Dartmouth. Meanwhile John Hawley mobilised his forces who were sent to meet the French. It is possible that the small stream which runs into the sea was a tidal creek at that time, so as it was high tide it formed a natural barrier between the opposing armies. The conflict was bloody but fortunately ended up in a 'home win'. Du Chatel was killed, as were many of his knights, whilst the surviving troops made a hasty retreat.

Nature has not always been at peace at Blackpool. The elements have been responsible for greatly changing the appearance of the beach at times. In 1869 strong gales removed the covering of sand from the south western end of the beach to reveal a clay deposit with many tree stumps embedded within. This is a submerged forest and is evidence of changes in sea levels. The unstable nature of the cliffs has also been a concern for many years.

In 1966 it was found necessary to protect the beach by placing blocks of hard, resistant green dolorite hewn from a quarry at East Allington (some six miles inland) and pinkish limestones extracted from Plymstock, many miles away to the west.

But enough of doom and gloom. Blackpool Sands is a wonderful haven, well sheltered from the prevailing winds and not over commercialised. In the morning sunshine, on a summer's day, it is 'Paradise' – and this comes from someone who is not obliged to write in the style of a tourist brochure writer! Film makers have appreciated the striking scenery. In *Ordeal By Innocence*, a film based on a story by Agatha Christie, there were sequences shot in this area, and in *Made in Devon* there is a photograph showing actor Donald Sutherland here. At nearby Strete, John Thaw (of *Inspector Morse* fame) portrayed Sir Francis Drake for a film, the cliffs of Devon playing the part of the South American coastline – no problem!

Strete is small with a population of about 500 and, like Stoke Fleming, occupies

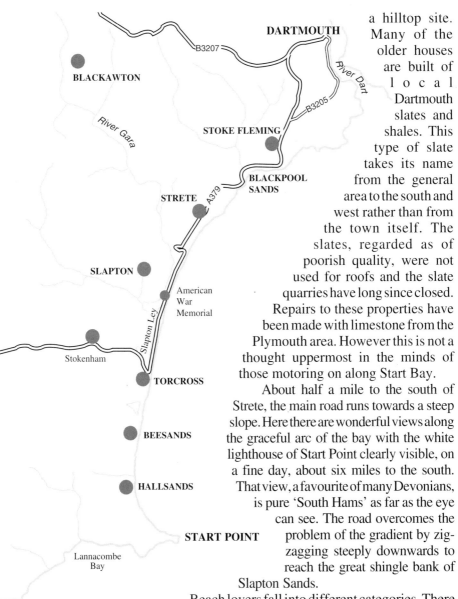

a hilltop site. Many of the older houses are built of local Dartmouth slates and shales. This type of slate takes its name from the general area to the south and west rather than from the town itself. The slates, regarded as of poorish quality, were not used for roofs and the slate quarries have long since closed. Repairs to these properties have been made with limestone from the Plymouth area. However this is not a thought uppermost in the minds of those motoring on along Start Bay.

About half a mile to the south of Strete, the main road runs towards a steep slope. Here there are wonderful views along the graceful arc of the bay with the white lighthouse of Start Point clearly visible, on a fine day, about six miles to the south. That view, a favourite of many Devonians, is pure 'South Hams' as far as the eye can see. The road overcomes the problem of the gradient by zig-zagging steeply downwards to reach the great shingle bank of Slapton Sands.

Beach lovers fall into different categories. There are those who love the gentle sloping sandy beaches where the tide goes out so far that you can hardly see the sea. Then there are those more sedate folk who go for the shingle or pebble beaches which have a much steeper profile and are generally less crowded. And there is a third variety of beach lover that we often forget – the geologist. To him it is the beach itself which is the fascination and in the case of Slapton Sands he will have much to gaze upon in

13

wonderment. Take a handful of Slapton's shingle, at random, and you will have materials in the palm of your hand which have come from many different pre-historic periods, also from a great number of locations.

Although the overall colour of the beach is golden, a closer examination of the beach material will show white fragments of flint, the rock which gave Stone-age man material for tools, weapons and for firemaking. Flint is common in East Devon and has in more recent times been an important raw material in the manufacture of bathroom and kitchen tiles, an historical nicety missed by the likes of Fred Flintstone and his megalithic mates.

However these flint particles come from the west and from the sea bed in the area near the Eddystone Lighthouse off Plymouth. There are more local materials like the dark coloured mica schists, which occur in a band across the southernmost headlands of Devon. Skimming slates across the water is an absorbing pastime on Slapton Beach, with slates found in the beach deposits ideal for record breaking attempts – who says Geology is dull?

The central part of southern Devon is dominated by Dartmoor which is a great dome of granite. The River Dart flowing from the moor has transported fragments of this rock, which was formed about 300 million years ago, down into Start Bay. In addition to this there are many other types of rock – limestone, chalk, various quartzes and so on.

The shingle beach, which begins at Strete Gate, is continuous for many miles. This twenty or so feet high wall of shingle has blocked off the flow of several streams which once ran unimpeded straight down into Start Bay. Consequently the shingle bank has provided a natural dam and ponded back behind it are a number of lakes which are referred to as leys in this area. At Slapton there is the

Higher Ley, Slapton Ley and Lower Ley. There are further smaller examples to the south at Beesands with Widdecombe Ley and at Greenstraight near Hallsands.

The River Gara originally entered Start Bay at Strete Gate but the shingle spit of Slapton Sands means that it now reaches the sea via a cavernous, almost secret, pipe beneath the village of Torcross some two and a half miles to the south.

Slapton Ley is a nature reserve, particularly important for its bird and fish life. Being on an east facing coastline it receives flocks of starlings, coot and duck from the Low Countries, particularly when they experience severe winters. However it is the autumn which sees many migrating flocks make a courtesy call.

The fishing at Slapton has always been good, perhaps no better than in 1905 when two gentleman, who were staying at the Torcross Hotel, managed to bag 21 pike and an amazing 1,812 perch and rudd in a four day stay. It should be stressed that these were caught by rod and not net. Sea angling is also a popular activity, evident by its many stalwart supporters who spend endless hours in pursuit of a specimen fish and who are willing to do so in the most atrocious conditions. To combat this they take along enough equipment and provisions to stave off a siege. Each to his own. At least, in theory, this end of Start Bay is partly sheltered from the prevailing south westerly winds.

A Sherman tank was positioned in the car park in Torcross, at the southern end of Slapton Ley, as a poignant reminder of six months' history when this quiet part of England was rudely awoken from its slumbers by an 'invading' army of American allies. In order to thoroughly prepare for the Normandy landings it was decided that a similar area should be commandeered so that a full dress rehearsal could take place. The coastline of Start Bay was ideal for the purpose, bearing a striking resemblance to the Cotentin Peninsula with its lagoons, marshes and undulating topography. In all, nine areas of Britain were taken over and this one, which comprised 30,000 acres and included many South Hams villages, was of great importance.

Like all things in wartime there was little time to dwell on too many fine points, the area was needed and the 3,000 people who lived in it had to go – within an absolute maximum of six weeks. The situation was made more complicated by the fact that everything had to be removed, including crops! This was a productive agricultural area which had been doing everything it could for the war effort already. Put yourself in their situation – farm animals, machinery, possessions, in fact anything which was not fixed, had to go.

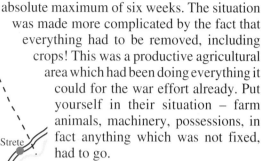

Some 750 families were involved and in many cases the fittest, strongest and most able members of families were already away at war. The news was broken to the residents in mid November 1943 and they had until 20 December to be out. The Devonshire climate showed little sympathy or understanding and the short, precious daylight hours were scenes of great activity. The incessant rain turned the lanes into mud baths. Helpers coming in from outside the area, unfamiliar with these surroundings, were often bamboozled in their attempts to reach their destinations, all signs having been removed so as not to help any foreign invaders!

There was a particular concern for the fabric of the many churches in the evacuated zone and much attention was given to moving out and disassembling any church furniture which might be at risk, because live ammunition was to be used in several frighteningly realistic exercises. Some of the churches still have bullet marks on them. Despite sandbagging, the placement of barbed wire and a moving written request from the Bishop of Exeter, which was pinned to each church, there was still much damage. In particular Blackawton fared badly but it

is believed that the wanton destruction which took place everywhere in the area was not solely the work of American troops. Between their eventual departure and the official re-opening, many trespassers and looters took advantage of the opportunity which arose for them to plunder and vandalise with little risk of being caught.

For many of the American troops who came to this quiet corner of Devon it was to be their last days; many hundreds were killed and stories which only came to light years afterwards continued to increase the death toll. Seven hundred and forty nine men of the US Navy and Army were killed when a convoy of landing ships was on an exercise out in the bay. A group of German E-boats, out of Cherbourg, sank a heavily-laden American craft, a massive disaster which, at the time, was hushed up for a number of reasons.

The Sherman tank at Torcross, unbeknown to its crew, was damaged to such an extent that when they launched it into the sea, from a landing craft, it plummeted to the sea bed in a depth of water of about 60 feet or ten fathoms. Fortunately all of its crew escaped to fight another day. Divers from Fort Bovisand, near Plymouth, managed to salvage it in 1984.

The obelisk which stands at the top of the beach at the northern end of Slapton Ley tends to get passed by holidaymakers, unaware of the significance of this area and its activities in World War II.

The monument was presented by the USA and unveiled on 24 July 1954. Everyone who was evacuated and who had returned were invited. Among the many military dignitaries to attend was General Alfred M Gruenther who later that day met many of the people who were involved in the drama a decade earlier. The war has long since gone, but every year many hundreds of Americans visit this area to see for themselves where their loved ones died.

The obelisk stands alone beside a large car park, a space which, prior to the planned conflict of late 1943 and early 1944, was the site of the Royal Sands Hotel, a large, well known but sprawling establishment. This was undamaged before the arrival of the troops but blown to smithereens in an exercise and was never rebuilt. It is believed that a stray dog inadvertently triggered a mine planted in the buildings.

The next village down the coastline beyond Torcross was just outside the zone which was commandeered. Beesands is a small fishing village with only a vestige left of what was a thriving fishing industry. The beach used to be strewn with fishing nets, pots and boats and was a colourful, highly animated scene a century ago. Today the hubbub of noise and excitement that accompanied the sound of returning fishermen has gone. What a struggle it was for them to get ashore as the currents of Start Bay run parallel to the beach and shoot towards Start Point. To remedy this problem powerful Newfoundland dogs were kept, these swam out with a rope to enable the boats to be winched ashore.

Beesands is an idyllic spot where it is possible to sit on the beach, in the lee of westerlies, beneath the great protective mounds of boulders placed there to defend the village against the occasional easterly bombardment of wind and tide.

A visit to the Cricket Inn, strategically and handily placed for the purchase of liquid refreshments, will reveal the problems this small community has faced in times past. On the wall are pictures and press cuttings showing such events as the storms of January 1979 when waves did immense damage at Torcross and went over the tops of the houses at Beesands! The landlord has kept a scrapbook of pictures which show just how vulnerable this coastline is under certain, but fortunately infrequent, conditions.

The Cricket Inn only survives courtesy of the summer trade – Beesands is almost a ghost village in winter. Many of the cottages along its strand are either second homes or holiday homes and are empty through the long winter months. There are few employment opportunities in the immediate vicinity and the roads out of the village must have been designed by a drunk and built by a sadist.

However, the cliff walk to the ruined village of Hallsands is pleasant, apart from a few squelchy sections, and less demanding on the nerves than the drive around to this fascinating place.

The more time that passes by the greater the imagination needs to be to envisage what Hallsands must have been like in its heyday. With each new season the derelict remains of this former fishing village diminish and, accordingly, it becomes more difficult, in the mind's eye, to see the quaint narrow main street, built on a narrow wave cut platform above the beach but beneath the cliffs, and the thirty seven dwellings that once comprised Hallsands.

The story of Hallsands is one which is familiar to most Devonians but one that is always told to illustrate man's folly in tampering with nature. In late Victorian times this was a village of about one hundred and fifty residents. So close knit was the community that villagers rarely locked their front doors and people wandered at will from house to house, as did the totally liberated free range hens which were kept to supplement the diet. However, the locals looked to the sea for their

livelihood, and at that time the regular migrating shoals of fish, plus the great resident population of lobsters and crabs lurking in the relatively shallow waters of Start Bay, enabled them to survive and thrive. Despite its small population the village boasted a blacksmith, carpenter and tailor so it was more or less self contained with its post office, a shop and the London Inn. This choice of name for the inn is interesting because Hallsands could have so easily been on a different planet to London. The main contact with the outside world would have been with the pleasure steamers which regularly called in for afternoon tea or refreshments whilst plying along the coast.

So far I have painted an almost idyllic picture of a village where the pace of life was in tandem with the gentle rising and falling of the tide. However, as the century drew to a close this tranquillity and settled existence was rudely shattered by a menacing intruder, one which was ultimately to cause the death of this village.

Many miles to the west at Devonport, the Royal Navy wished to extend Devonport's dockyard frontage, a scheme which required vast amounts of shingle for concrete. Sir John Jackson Ltd won the tender for this job and, knowing of the

ideal availability of shingle in Start Bay, they applied to the Board of Trade for a licence to dredge the required shingle. The locals shook their heads in disbelief and knew no good would come of it. But they were assured that the natural anti-clockwise cycle of currents of Start Bay would replace the shingle, or at least compensate the shortfall so dredging began, in earnest, in April 1897. Each day 1,600 tons of shingle was removed, initially from below Tinsey Head to the north of the village. The first removals took place above the low water mark and below the high water mark (this being the geographical definition of a beach). Later shingle was taken from the sea bed.

Now beaches are important features in the landscape. Apart from their obvious charm to sit upon, sunbathe or stroll along they fulfil a vital role in protecting the coastline. They act as a cushion against all the might and power that the sea can throw at them. In the case of Hallsands and Beesands they absorbed all the wave attacks that winds of a generally easterly direction could throw at them. When the prevailing westerlies blew there were few problems as Beesands and Hallsands were sheltered at such times. However, this beach, where the fishermen tended to their nets or hauled in their catches, changed greatly as the dredgers sucked away the shingle. The beach level fell by many feet which meant that every time there were strong onshore easterly winds, the village was left exposed to a destructive sea.

Wilson's Rock, which is prominent on the beach at Hallsands, barely poked through the shingle in Victorian times. In the autumnal storms of 1900 the stone sea wall was demolished and the sand and gravel held in behind it to give it strength was washed away with consummate ease. Several of the properties on the seaward side of the street collapsed at the same time. After many protests, and a lengthy delay, the Board of Trade cancelled the licence for dredging in 1902 but the damage had already been done. Although compensation was forthcoming, it wasn't enough.

More repairs were made, a new sea wall was constructed and for several years it appeared that they would save the tiny community. The optimism coincided with a span of seasons when the weather conditions, that is not too many easterlies, favoured the villagers. However Richard Hansford-Worth, engineer of the sea wall, feared that certain conditions could end in disaster. On 26 January 1917 his worst fears were confirmed.

In anticipation of a storm, the fishermen had hauled their boats as high above the water line as they could. The first houses to be washed away were those which had been built over chasms on the rocky ledge. By midnight four houses had been totally removed and at daybreak the villagers, who had been penned back by high seas and prevented from climbing the cliff path to safety, took advantage of a low tide and lull in the storm. Amazingly much of the sea wall had held but only one house remained habitable.

The good old *Western Morning News* championed the right for decent compensation. Local dignitaries also threw their weight into the campaign. In the meantime some of the villagers went to stay with relatives, whilst some stayed in nearby barns and some really unfortunate folk even had to sleep amongst the ruins. It took years to resolve their housing problems but a line of dwellings called

'Fordworth Cottages' was built on the side of the Bickerton Valley, a short distance from the original settlement, sufficiently high above sea level to be safe. They were named after Hansford Worth and H. Ford who both did much for the plight of the villagers. Mr Worth will also be remembered for his great love of Dartmoor and his wonderful writings and researches on this subject.

Today people make the pilgrimage to visit the atmospheric but ever diminishing deserted village. There is a small free car park a little distance away and refreshments are available at Prospect House (pictured on previous page) which was originally Trout's Hotel. The Trouts are a locally famous family with long established connections with fishing and the sea. In 1917 Ella Trout was likened to Grace Darling as when she was out crabbing she saw a cargo ship being torpedoed. Ella rowed over a mile out to sea to rescue a young man, a deed that earned her an OBE and a substantial financial reward from the young man's grateful parents.

The sea continues to nibble away at this bit of coastline and the properties on the cliff top keep a vigilant eye on the receding cliff. The derelict chapel dangles precariously and is not too far away from a final 'Amen', and the coast path has been rerouted. Nearby the school (for want of a better word) has been converted to domestic use.

Just a little inland is the hamlet of Huckham where the school today is owned by Exmouth's Comprehensive School and is used as a fieldwork centre. It provides a lot of young Exmothians with a chance to see a part of the county which is so very different to their own 'civilised', more urban environment.

From a literary, or even a geographical, standpoint it seems a contradiction in terms to actually get to 'the Start' after so many pages! However, for ages now we have been staring at Start Point lighthouse, its light guiding Channel shipping since 1836. This headland is most distinctive with its great piles of hard gneiss rocks tapering downwards to the lighthouse. Its name derives from the Anglo Saxon word 'steort' which means a tail. It certainly bears a tail-like resemblance of some reptilian monster. (It looks a bit like a lizard but the Cornish were quicker off the mark to use that name.) Co-incidentally, geologically this part of Devon has similarities with Cornwall's Lizard peninsular and both are in the southernmost areas of their respective counties.

The lighthouse has a range of just over twenty miles and its light flashes out with the equivalent of 800,000 candlepower. The main lamp is normally expected to last about a thousand hours, yet the one installed in 1873 finally flickered out some eighty seven 'light' years later in 1960. For many years it was possible to enjoy a guided tour of the lighthouse, but automation of the lighthouse has put paid to this.

Someone who would not have appreciated the joys and delights of the great view along Start Bay from the headland was Henry Muge. This unfortunate pirate was executed on Start Point and his corpse was left dangling in chains as a stark reminder to passing seamen not to get involved in skullduggery on the seas. Some

say on stormy nights that they can hear the rattling of his bones!

The dreadful currents which meet from different directions often combine to produce difficult seas, even in relatively calm weather. Bathing is regarded as highly dangerous in the immediate vicinity and old sea salts swear that the long-since departed spirits of drowned seamen meet here.

On a happier note, several years ago, Graham Ibbertson, a lighthouse keeper at Start Point, along with his wife, decided to have the rest of his family baptised, ninety steps up, in the lamproom of the lighthouse. The Rev. Donald Peyton-Jones, who in his role of Chaplain to the Seamen's Mission had already performed similar services on oil rigs and beaches, conducted the ceremony. It was believed to be a first on mainland Britain so was recorded for posterity by a local television company. Symbolically the light was switched on to mark the occasion, replacing the normal candle evident at more conventional christenings.

From Start Point to the mouth of the Salcombe or Kingsbridge Estuary is a stretch of spectacular coastline which can be walked on the coastal footpath. It is probably the most enjoyable section of coastwalking in Devon and, if you have the energy to cope with the constant roller-coaster nature of the cliff path, you will be well rewarded. If you are incapable, then I hope you can gain some appreciation and enjoyment from the stories and photographs included in this little book.

The coastline changes direction at Start Point. Below the coastpath is the beautiful beach of Great Mattiscombe Sand which locals pronounce "Matchcum". For the next few miles the coastpath follows a flat, narrow bench-like surface with low cliffs on the seaward side and steep rocky outcrops on the landward side. It all makes for an impressive stroll onto Lannacombe where the remains of a watermill may be traced, and until recently two solid granite millstones lay on the sands.

Lannacombe is a beach but not a resort. It has a few car spaces but these are soon occupied on fine days. In the best interests of the local residents who have to use the narrow twisty lanes leading down to this lovely little spot, it may be better to leave Lannacombe to its loyal band of regular patrons.

The coastline goes on heading ever southwards until it reaches Prawle Point and then it can travel southwards no further as this is Devon's southernmost point. On top of the headland is a small building which was a Lloyds signal station, an important telegraph link with London in the past.

The distinctive-looking coastguard cottages, just below Prawle Point, were the scene of a most violent incident in 1872. An Italian vessel had gone aground at Lannacombe and the survivors were accommodated at a nearby village pub. However the 'demon drink' got the better of one of the Italians and in an ugly argument he pulled out a knife and stabbed several of his shipmates. In the absence of a policeman (there was little need of one in this area and probably still isn't) a coastguard was summoned and he too was stabbed. The Italian, still in a state of high excitement, ran to the coastguard cottages to vent his anger on other coastguards and even a coastguard's wife. A frantic struggle was terminated when the Italian was killed by a coastguard officer wielding a cutlass.

The coastline for the few miles, between Prawle Point and the mouth of the Kingsbridge Estuary, near Salcombe, is superb. It includes the strikingly beautiful Gammon Head and has many other features which have a meaty South 'Hams' connection: The Bull, The Pig's Nose and The Ham Stone are just three of the ones to appear on the OS Map.

Like so many miles of coastline in the South West, the National Trust own this section and the path is well looked after. The only place of refreshment, between Prawle and East Portlemouth, on the coast walk, is The Gara Rock Hotel which was formerly a row of coastguard cottages known as the Rickham Coastguard Station.

The 1851 census revealed that 41 people lived here, of whom eight were coastguards. Their look-out post, an upright cylindrical-shaped building, was converted into a bar in 1971 and may well have qualified as the smallest one in the world, but it closed at the end of its first summer. Several famous people have been drawn to Gara Rock because of its striking cliff top location – amongst these were the late Sir John Betjeman, Sir Laurence Olivier and Margaret Rutherford. Another well known actor, Nigel Havers, came to Gara Rock to shoot some sequences for the television series *A Horseman Riding By*. This was adapted from the book written by R.F. Delderfield who lived at Sidmouth in East Devon. At various times photographic fashion models have descended on Gara Rock to demonstrate their particular art form with the stunning South Hams scenery as a backcloth.

Beyond this distinctive hotel the coastal path winds it way along the edge of Rickham Common, where there used to be a golf course, before entering the sheltered Kingsbridge Estuary. The path skirts numerous small beaches of clear, golden sand and, seen on a fine sunny day, there is probably no prettier picture in the whole of England!

It leads to East Portlemouth, opposite Salcombe, or at least to the pedestrian ferry which lies at the foot of the hill beneath this small village. A long and steep flight of steps rises up towards the church, proving to be a genuine test of stamina! But it is well worth the effort for the view is awesome, with Kingsbridge and much of distant Dartmoor in view. It is hard to imagine that this peaceful place was once such a den of smuggling that the preventive men were obliged to demolish two public houses in order to restrict such illegal practices.

By dividing the ferry tariff across to Salcombe by the number of metres you travel, it will be discovered that this works out to be one of the most expensive journeys in the world. However, the season is short and whichever way you travel it's well worth every penny. The alternative is a drive of about 17 miles!

Salcombe, in terms of population, is a lot smaller than many would imagine, only just about topping the two thousand mark. In high summer the numbers double and Devon's southernmost settlement really comes alive. However it is in winter when the sheltered nature of Salcombe's location enables it to boast the mildest climate in the area. Some well intentioned writers and brochure compilers have been known to exaggerate this point and wild claims have been made about 'never needing to wear a heavy coat'. The celebrated historian, Anthony Froude, who spent his final years in Salcombe, wrote that "the winter of Salcombe is winter only in name." People who imagine that this is a tropical haven should look at the average, or mean, figures which reveal that, whilst the town is marginally warmer than many other places, it is not as warm in winter as it is often suggested. It can sustain sub-tropical, exotic plants mainly because of its very sheltered position in the lee of the prevailing winds – it is protected by high cliffs and hills.

It is the sheltered nature of the estuary which has been instrumental in this area developing into such a popular spot for the yachting fraternity. To the north of Salcombe the estuary opens up to an amazing series of finger-like creeks, most of which end abruptly with small hamlets or villages at the head of them. This is a sailing paradise and had this book not been written by a dedicated, non-swimming landlubber, more space and even greater appreciation would have been given over to the undoubted delights to be enjoyed in this superb estuary. Those of such a persuasion should acquire and read *Under Sail Through South Devon and Dartmoor* by Raymond B. Cattell because it is a beautifully chronicled look at this area as seen from the water.

Historically this estuary has also been much used for all sorts of purposes, some of which were not too wholesome. In the seventeenth century it was a safe haven for pirates, and it was not unknown for the local fishermen to supplement their income with a spot of smuggling, an activity which was synonymous with the entire coastline of the south-west peninsular.

Intermingled with illegal practices were the fine sailing ships of the past, the Salcombe Clippers which ranged in size from 100 to 500 tons and whose speed

was of paramount importance in bringing back cargoes of oranges, pineapples and other perishable products from the Azores, the Mediterranean and the West Indies. At its peak Salcombe had a thousand seamen, and a great many clippers which had to be built, fitted out, maintained and equipped, either in Salcombe or at Kingsbridge, at the head of the estuary.

The clippers carried names like *Salcombe Castle, Erme* (named after the lovely river which runs into the western side of Bigbury Bay), *Malborough* (an important hilltop village on the main road to Kingsbridge), *Lord Devon* and *Queen of the South*. There were many others and each of these Salcombe fruiterers must have made an impressive spectacle with their tall masts, well kept hulls, smart canvas and everything kept scraped and varnished – all ship-shape and Salcombe fashion.

These were resilient craft even in troubled waters, particularly the tea clippers when a storm was 'brewing'.

In order to get the best out of the London market, they returned from their long journeys as quickly and as anonymously as possible. That is, of course, until they were under London Bridge. Then it was the practice to select the largest pineapple on board and attach it to the end of the jib boom, a blatant promotional act to herald their arrival in port. Back in the home port of Salcombe, the entire waterfront was a scene of vessels crowding in two abreast.

After their long journey, maintenance work was often required as the vessels came home with such cargoes as tobacco, cocoa and coffee from Puerto Rico; lime juice and spices from Dominica; sugar and ginger from Barbados; timber, cotton and fruit from the United States; yet more coffee, grain and meat from South America; oranges from the Azores; and oil, marble and wine from various Mediterranean countries. The mouth-watering array of items made the Salcombe waterfront a colourful spectacle.

To keep the armada of ships afloat, boatyards, blacksmiths, sailmakers and ropemakers sprang up creating a rapid growth in the middle of the nineteenth century. In order to sustain the needs of the boatyards, a great many oak trees were felled in the woods around Kingsbridge. These were taken down to the estuary and then towed by rowing boat down to Salcombe. Although this sounds a straightforward enough exercise, it was a potentially dangerous occupation. Four local men drowned in 1837 and their bodies were discovered on the estuary mud as the tide receded. This incident so upset the local community that, at their funeral, over two thousand mourners turned up to pay their last respects.

The hard won timber was sawn by sawyers in pits by the water's edge where there was much activity. Along the waterfront could be heard the constant sounds of caulking mallets, the air pervaded with the smell of pitch and tar to complete

the scene of a busy, bustling small South Devon port.

However, in far-off places, great engineers, like Brunel, were experimenting with iron ships and steam ships and the days of the Salcombe clippers were numbered. One by one these wonderful little wooden ships were sold and went on to perform other, perhaps less exciting, tasks as Salcombe wasn't sheltered from this particular wind, the wind of change. Cardiff-built freighters usurped the trade of the Salcombe clippers and slowly the shipyards fell into disrepair and Salcombe slipped into a slumberous period when the only vessels seen were the occasional coal barge or that carrying stone from one of the many quarries in or around the creeks of the Kingsbridge Estuary.

Others though may argue that such a lovely spot as Salcombe was better off without the trappings of trade and maritime industry. Lincolnshire-born poet, Tennyson, enjoyed its mixture of bustle combined with beauty. His *Crossing the Bar* (not the sort you find in a pub) is based on the dangerous submarine ridge at the mouth of the estuary on which many a mariner has met with misfortune. Another of his poems was *The Lotus Eaters,* a majestic piece of poetry. The ancient Greeks made a wine from lotus leaves producing an elixir which induced a sense of happy, oblivion, a feeling which was not too far removed from the great thinkers, philosophers and poets who chose to take up temporary residence in Salcombe.

The inevitable progression continued as those with money and time on their hands began to enjoy sailing. This, of course, has become the stock-in-trade of the town and has largely come to dominate the scene.

However, let us not forget the ordinary local folk who don't necessarily have the time to mess around in boats. Spare a thought for poor Sally Stone, who can claim the distinction of becoming Salcombe's first Postmistress in 1821, regarded as being quite an honour. In order to obtain this position she had to walk, every day for several years, to Kingsbridge and back to deliver letters on the return journey.

When this all got too much for her, she took to making the more direct journey up the estuary in a rowing boat, which she did in all weathers. She even had the necessary pulling power to accommodate not only the parcels that she collected but passengers as well. She truly earned her post as Postmistress and the grand salary of £5 per year that went with it.

It is possibly something in the air, or in the water, that has made Salcombe folk very determined, or stubborn, in their ways. Salcombe Castle, now known as Fort Charles, is a relic of an amazing act of defiance during the English Civil War. As the conflict drew to an end, this little outpost held out for the Royalist cause. Despite four months of continual bombardment, in which only one person from either side was killed, the Royalists in Fort Charles still refused to surrender. The situation was resolved, at the very end of the Civil War, when the sixty six men and two laundresses were allowed to march out bearing their arms, beating their drums and with their colours flying – a dignified and gracious ending to the prolonged siege.

The resident chaplain at Fort Charles was John Snell, who was Rector of nearby Thurlestone. It had been agreed that he should return to his village to carry on his normal duties, but he had his cattle stolen and life was made so unbearable that he had to flee the area. He remained in exile until the Restoration when he was well compensated by being made a canon of Exeter Cathedral.

By late Victorian times, when the railway network had spread all across Devon, Salcombe had to decide whether it wanted a rail link with Kingsbridge and thus the rest of civilisation. When all the pros and cons had been sufficiently weighed, a vote was taken in the town and, by a healthy majority, it was decided against such a proposal. With an absence of railways and no dual carriageways within many miles, Salcombe has managed to stave off the mass development other more accessible resorts have experienced. Locals will no doubt say that the town isn't what it was like in the past, but that is the case everywhere. However, it is

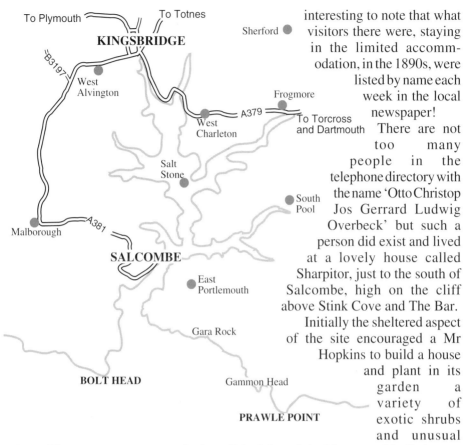

interesting to note that what visitors there were, staying in the limited accommodation, in the 1890s, were listed by name each week in the local newspaper! There are not too many people in the telephone directory with the name 'Otto Christop Jos Gerrard Ludwig Overbeck' but such a person did exist and lived at a lovely house called Sharpitor, just to the south of Salcombe, high on the cliff above Stink Cove and The Bar.

Initially the sheltered aspect of the site encouraged a Mr Hopkins to build a house and plant in its garden a variety of exotic shrubs and unusual trees. The next owners promptly demolished the original house and built the one that stands there today. However they carried on Hopkins' work and continued to develop the gardens by introducing new species.

Mr Overbeck bought the estate in 1928. He was a research chemist and was also a collector of all sorts of things. He died in 1937 and bequeathed the house, the grounds and his collections to the National Trust. The house was to be a youth hostel, the grounds open for people to enjoy and the museum there for the enjoyment and education of all. Children will enjoy going through a secret door but I won't tell you what lies behind it because Sharpitor is one of those places you must visit for yourself.

The six acre sub-tropical garden possesses a prized magnolia, Japanese banana palms, olive, camphor, a maidenhair tree from China and many other examples of flora normally associated with warmer climes.

To enjoy the next stretch of coastline you really have to be a rambler and, from Sharpitor onwards, an energetic one for it is quite a long haul up to Sharp Tor and then on and around to Bolt Head. On a fine morning this is an amazing experience but well worth any beads of sweat that may moisten the brow. The views from these towering cliffs are spectacular and it is from this vantage point that it is easiest to appreciate the awful plight of the *Herzogin Cecilie* which was eventually beached at Starehole Bay at the base of Bolt Head in 1936.

On a coastline where hundreds of ships have been lost this particular shipwreck had an unusual background – it was a disaster that was not altogether unexpected.

The captain's wife, Mrs Eriksson, had had a nightmare that the ship had gone on the rocks so begged her husband not to leave Falmouth for Ipswich. Despite her many pleas he set sail, with her, and a crew of about 30 aboard, probably dismissing the dream as an occupational hazard for a seaman's spouse. However, this 3,000 ton vessel, which had a long history of maritime misfortune, a most unlucky ship, did go on the rocks near Sewer Mill Cove. She was then miles off course and in his ensuing report the captain stated that a combination of factors were responsible. Amongst the reasons cited for going aground was that a possible magnetic attraction by the cliffs may have thrown the ship's compass out.

Following the arrival of the Salcombe lifeboat, most of the crew were taken off. The captain, his good lady and some of the crew, stayed aboard. The custom men who came aboard impounded all alcohol and cigarettes and even killed a pet pig. Having tossed its carcass into the sea, they were then haunted by it for several days as it kept floating past!

Personal possessions were taken ashore by a breeches buoy, only to be immediately stolen by members of the public at the other end, thereby keeping up a tradition harking back to the days of 'wreckers'. It seems that everybody tried to get in on the act of gaining from the misfortune of others. Some of the landowners were wise to the fact that hundreds of people were coming down to see the world's biggest windjammer, and a kingly toll was extracted for the privilege, 'a nice little earner' as they say – and all this in an age when life was supposed to be less mercenary and not as materialistic as it is today!

It was months before she was refloated and taken to Stairhole Cove where she sank into sand some twelve feet deep. A month after this a south easterly gale created a strong sea that broke her back. Everything which could be salvaged was taken away and a Kingsbridge scrap metal dealer bought the wreck which, over the following three years, was broken by the elements into four distinct parts.

The old town of Kingsbridge is set on rising ground and the main street leading up from the estuary is steep enough to render most senior citizens breathless, however, many retired folk have chosen this as their final haven. It is an ideal spot at the head of the many fingered Kingsbridge Estuary, which is a classic example of a feature called a ria or submerged river valley.

To many, if you mention Kingsbridge and forget to include Dodbrooke it can cause offence. Dodbrooke has merged with it yet at one time it was a borough in its own right. As Eric Morecombe often said, "You can't see the join."

The name 'King's Bridge' probably refers to a bridge which, according to records, existed in a charter of 962, linking two royal estates. The settlement, later developed by an abbot of Buckfast, was therefore aptly named.

Kingsbridge (which by implication includes Dodbrooke) has always been a busy little town. The early corn mill in the town was converted in 1798 in order that woollen goods could be manufactured for the East India Company. When this trade subsided the mill turned to blankets and other woollen items which were sent as far afield as Newfoundland, an environment known for its rigorous winter climate. During the Great Blizzard of 1891 the locals would have been glad of winter woollies themselves as Kingsbridge was completely cut off for six weeks. However, by then it had reverted to a corn mill again. It finally closed in 1967 and was pulled down in 1984.

The waterfront scene has also been a busy area with a flourishing fruit trade,

which lasted until the end of the nineteenth century. There were shipyards which included those run by Mr Date who built fruit clippers and trawlers for the Plymouth and Brixham fleets. Kingsbridge also was the birthplace of many steamers such as *The Kingsbridge Packet* and *The Queen*. The latter replaced the rowing boats which formerly plied between Kingsbridge and Salcombe. It did poor Edward Woods out of a livelihood whilst at the same time broke the hearts of many of the young ladies of these estuary towns. Young Edward not only had roguish good looks but also a twinkle in his eye that melted the hearts of the young ladies, some of whom would pay for the ride simply to spend some time in his company! *The Queen* was considerably larger than the rowing boats and when the tides were too low it had to disembark its passengers further down the estuary. The passengers then had to climb a steep bank before trooping along the side of the creek into Kingsbridge town.

On arrival they no doubt had acquired a mighty thirst. Fortunately there were many brewers in the town and their cider was celebrated far and wide as a tasty and potent brew. However it is the 'white ale' to which all the guide books refer. It was a rare old brew which contained eggs, pepper, spices, milk and gin. In summer locals added ginger beer but it is believed the main ingredient was 'grout'. Why anyone ever drunk it should be the question for, by all accounts, it was an evil mix, best left well alone. It was rumoured by the ancient wise men of the town that a man whose constitution could stand one gulp would have nothing more to fear from the ravages of time, and that constant imbibing of this brew would guarantee long life. This example of early advertising hype shows why we need the Advertising Standards Authority!

A close look at the ordnance survey map of the district will reveal many disused quarries which at one time offered employment to many of the townsfolk. High quality slate was the main product and vast amounts were shipped down the estuary, much of it heading towards Plymouth or Torbay. It was far easier to convey almost any item by sea, particularly heavy materials like this as the lanes around the South Hams are not suitable for speedy or easy transport.

The first stage coach to enter Kingsbridge, on a regular basis, was in 1824 running southwards down from South Brent. It was instigated to offer a connecting service with the main Exeter to Plymouth route.

The journey from Kingsbridge to Wrangaton, all of twelve miles, took two and a quarter hours. It was not always without incident. On one occasion the driver got off to deliver a parcel and the driverless stage coach pulled off without him. It went several miles to Loddiswell where, without assistance, it made its customary stop.

The coming of the railway in December 1893, was many years later than most branch lines to the other towns in Devon. 'The Primrose Line' as it became known, followed the Aune, or Avon, valley for two thirds of its twelve and a half miles and was regarded as a superb ride up until its closure in 1963.

The River Avon meanders about its deep steep valley with so many twists and turns that the railway engineers were obliged to construct ten bridges over it. Amazingly, in just twelve miles of track there were forty eight bridges and a 640 yard tunnel beneath Sorley.

It is possible to appreciate some of its best scenery as now the railway has been dismantled, sections of it can be followed on foot. The most unattractive part of this railway is its terminus in Kingsbridge, now an industrial estate (or something along those lines!).

However, there is still a railway in Kingsbridge – albeit a miniature one – which runs alongside the Quay Car Park. 'Heidi' has been chugging along this water's edge stretch of seven and a quarter inch gauge railway since 1976. It has been estimated that she does well over a thousand miles each season so she has almost gone a distance sufficient to take her right around the world – without ever leaving Kingsbridge.

The line is the brainchild of hardworking Geoffrey Kitchenside, a man who

railway buffs will know for his many fine articles and books. With his wife he runs the Gorse Blossom Railway near Bickington, just off the main Exeter to Plymouth road.

There are certain things which you have to mention for each place and for Kingsbridge the historical detail which is most synonymous with the town is that it is the birthplace, in 1705, of William Cookworthy, who gives his name to the town's fine museum. William experimented with China Clay, his finds eventually leading to a major industry in Devon and Cornwall. English China Clay help to fund the museum which is full of surprises.

It is often said that Kingsbridge is the capital of The South Hams. It only had just over four thousand residents at the last census but, as all roads seem to lead here, and as there are no serious rivals, it seems to be a reasonable claim.

Kingsbridge witnessed an unusual but most special event in April 1991 when a locally trained horse returned to the South Hams, triumphant after winning the Grand National. Seagram, a relatively small horse, was publicly paraded at Kingsbridge, much to the delight of those who had backed the trusty steed which was trained by David Baron at Higher Hendham Farm some four miles to the north of the town.

The Salt Stone is an estuary reef about 100 feet long and fifty feet wide, situated half way between Kingsbridge and Salcombe. It lies a little offshore from Wareham Point, where the lovely Frogmore Creek unites with the main channel. At high tide the Salt Stone is covered but at low tide it is clearly visible. It was of great importance to non-conformists in the seventeenth century. Their form of worship had been outlawed and anyone practising their faith was persecuted. In order to celebrate their simple services of devotion, out of the way locations were chosen, the Salt Stone being a favoured spot as it was not in any parish.

However, so fervent were the worshippers that there were occasions when they were divinely distracted and failed to notice the rising tide which gave them a surprise baptism! Until 1930 a wooden cross was visible on this rock as a memorial to the seventeenth century worshippers.

Although Kingsbridge was regarded as a refuge, there were still those opposed to them. These people could earn a tidy sum by informing on the non-conformists. Heavy fines were imposed on those who broke the Act of Uniformity which had been passed in 1662. The informers received a third of any fines resulting from their information. Seventy three Ministers in Devon were expelled for non conforming and many of these settled in the South Hams. It was one of these, John Hicks, who conducted regular services on the Salt Stone. Other services were held in secluded woods or in disused quarry pits; these were ideal acoustically and also afforded some shelter in inclement weather. However they were less easy to escape from when cornered. Nevertheless the services drew big crowds in this area. The Declaration of Indulgence in 1687 saw the end of worship in such out of the way locations.

Another disused quarry used for this purpose, was located in this area at Ticket or Tacket Wood. The 'Ticket' was needed as proof of being a genuine worshipper and had to be handed in at the quarry entrance.

John Hicks was an interesting character. As his life moved on he grew increasingly tough and was known to set about anyone who was a threat. Eventually he had to flee the district, only to become entangled in the Monmouth uprising. Siding with James, Duke of Monmouth, our stalwart friend was at Sedgemoor in Somerset, when the Duke and his force were defeated. With two associates he escaped and went into hiding but, although by now he was something of an expert at this, he was discovered. The lady who had given refuge, ignorant of his part in the uprising, was executed, and John Hicks appeared before the dreaded and notorious Judge Jeffreys. He was sentenced to death and beheaded at Glastonbury on 3 October 1685.

Several South Hams churches are mentioned in this small book but perhaps the most unusual is that of St Andrew's Church at South Huish. Built in the thirteenth century, it served its small, agricultural community for six hundred years. However its condition deteriorated, the fateful death knell occurring during a Divine Service in 1866 when a window was blown in, almost killing the priest.

The abandoned church became overgrown and its fabric even more ruinous and unsafe. It seemed that this distinctive landmark would simply moulder away until 'The Friends of the Friendless Churches' arrived on the scene to carry out repairs to halt its decline. Consequently open air services have occasionally been conducted in the ruins.

Malborough is a hilltop village on the main road from Kingsbridge to Salcombe. The church tower of All Saints is the most obvious landmark of the central part of the South Hams and is clearly visible from many vantage points of Southern Dartmoor.

In August 1829 something strange happened here. A man who lay on his death bed, barely able to speak, managed to inform all in the room with him that, when he was dead, he should be buried before midday. He insisted that if this didn't happen there would be problems. He duly died a day later and arrangements for his funeral at All Saints were made. On the day of the funeral, the vicar was delivering his discourse on the dead man's attributes when midday struck. Almost simultaneously there was a loud thunderclap, accompanied by a lightning bolt which shook the church. So scared was the congregation that they fled from the church – with the priest at the head of the stampede. Fearing that a disaster, like the one at Widecombe in the Moor, might befall them, they took shelter in nearby houses. For the duration of several hours the storm raged all around the district with great bolts of lightning, thunder like cannon fire and a deluge of rain. All the while the coffin remained in the church alone, awaiting a Christian burial.

Sherford is a tiny village tucked away in the middle of nowhere, a few miles from Kingsbridge. Its church possesses an amazing cross which shines brilliantly bright on a dull day, defying any logic. There is a picture of it, taken without a flash in only average light, in *Tales of the Unexplained in Devon* by Judy Chard.

It is hard to imagine it now, but once, or perhaps twice, Bolberry Down, a mile or so to the south west of Malborough, was a sporting venue. This great high cliff-top plateau was the location for Kingsbridge Races, but to avoid penalties the event was officially called The Kingsbridge Annual Diversions, the top prize being less than £50 (but in 1770 this would have been a tidy sum of money). The sound of thudding hooves was transferred, first to Middle Soar Farm nearer to Salcombe and then on to East Allington several miles inland. Eventually this annual event, originally staged in June, moved to Totnes where, each September, it survived until the outbreak of the last war (1939). It is strange that Kingsbridge Races should become Totnes Races in such 'merry-go-roundabout' fashion.

In more recent times, but now also defunct, there was a nine hole golf course on Bolberry Down. It had a smart pavilion to accommodate both ladies and gentlemen, and there were plans to extend it to a fully-fledged 18 hole course. It's probably just as well that this never happened for there are already plenty of courses along this coastline where people out enjoying a coastal stroll have to be constantly on the look out for mishit golf books whizzing around their ears!

Not many people live in Hope but quite a few people would like to as it is a picturesque settlement tucked snugly into the south east corner of Bigbury Bay.

Despite its lack of size, it is divided into two settlements, Inner and Outer Hope. Inner has its chocolate-box appearance cottages and disused lifeboat station, whilst Outer has its shops and its beach. It has been known for many people enjoying regular holidays to Hope Cove to choose it as their retirement haven, and there has been a recent growth in the number of new homes and bungalows.

There is a marked contrast between the scene on a hot August beach day, when the smell of sun tan lotion wafts on the wind and the beaches are thronged with a mass of visitors, and the wild autumnal nights when the wind howls across Bigbury Bay battering this small community. On such nights Outer Hope is like a ghost town.

When Robbie Coltrane and the 'Comic Strip' team visited Hope to make the film *Supergrass* there was a strong sea running. The well-built actor had to walk

along the breakwater whilst large waves broke over him. Some months later I tried a similar stunt on a much less inclement day and almost came to grief as, in places, it is decidedly slippery!

Normally when a film is made on location it uses fictitious names, but in *Supergrass* Hope Cove retained its own identity. Perhaps it was felt that such a name sounded fictitious enough! Once again, though, we are treading on ground more fully covered in *Made in Devon*.

Hope's past is inextricably linked with the sea which has created its livelihood, but also on many occasions threatened its or its residents existence. Fishing was of paramount importance with the various migrating shoals of fish like pilchard providing an income. The unpolluted coastal waters were also ideal for crabs and lobsters, monsters of the deep which reached fearful sizes. And when the fishing became a little tedious there was always a little bit of relief with a spot of smuggling, a word synonymous with the entire South Devon and Cornish coastline. Sadly the best stories of practised deceit are lost in the memories of those men who braved dark nights to steal in to quiet coves, avoiding the gaze of the coastguard or the Preventive men. Brandy was the main illicit import but if it became spoilt by sea water it was called 'Stinkibus'.

The smugglers had their own jargon, a vocabulary which is interesting but infrequently heard these days. 'Stingo' was strong malt liquor whilst 'flaskers' were the smugglers who ran the goods. The smugglers themselves were 'The Gentlemen' who ventured out on 'Darks', moonless nights, to move a 'crop of goods'.

The trade was at its zenith in the eighteenth and early nineteenth centuries but as surveillance techniques and organisation improved, these nefarious activities reduced. Strangely it was not a crime to sell the smuggled goods. It all adds a bit of romance to the scene and it's easy to envisage what it must have been like in such a quiet and remote spot beneath the great arm and rocky fortress of Bolt Tail.

Bigbury Bay has been the graveyard of many ships and my little book *Burgh Island and Bigbury Bay* gives more detail. However the worst disaster of all time must be mentioned, albeit briefly, as 700 folk lost their lives just offshore from Hope Cove when HMS *Ramillies* went aground on Bolt Tail in 1760. It is believed that a navigational error was to blame, Burgh Island being wrongly taken for Looe Island many miles to the west. It was a most unfortunate end for a vessel which had survived for nearly a century, a real feat for ships at that time. She had come through almost every major sea confrontation possible but, ironically, perished through natural causes. Only about two dozen people survived and many of those sustained terrible injuries. The bay was awash with bodies the next day and many of them were never recovered. Indeed it was more than two centuries before a lot of her guns and possessions were salvaged. The tiny cove where it went aground is now named after the *Ramillies.*

The great high cliffs of Bolt Tail wrap their arm around Hope Cove in the shape of a bent elbow. This is the start of Bigbury Bay, a wide expanse of rugged coastline which, for many days of the year, braces itself against the impact of the prevailing south westerly wind.

This stretch of coastline is great for walking but anyone contemplating a route march along it will need to consider the obstacles at the mouths of the Rivers Avon and Erme which range from mildly daunting to impossible depending on tide and tempest.

Thurlestone has a pretty village main street with a prominent church at the end of it. It has grown out of proportion in recent years – and when seen from a distance the song 'Little Boxes' springs to mind.

But it is its little golf balls of which the wayfarer has to beware as the coastal path skirts the rim of some fairly low cliffs along the edge of the golf course. Signs indicate this aerial threat whilst another sign warns of the possible dangers of swimming in the sea near the sewage outlet – hopefully this second sign will soon become superfluous.

Thus far I have painted a picture of potential danger but this stretch to Bantham is beautiful and should not be missed. For most of the way along it the Thurle Stone's impressive arch can be seen a little offshore. Its name means 'holed stone'.

This resistant rock was supposed to reflect the hardiness of the local breed of women.

Bantham is one of the few extensive sandy beaches in the South Hams and has a line of convenient dunes at the back of it for those who seek shelter or privacy. On a fine Sunday in high summer its expansive car parks fill to overflowing and a wide estimate would suggest that as many as two or three thousand cars might find their way there. Indeed Bantham's beach is revered by many as their favourite place. Just up the road is the small hamlet of Bantham which has 'The Sloop' as its pub.

A walk across the former Iron-Age settlement of Bantham Ham leads to the mouth of the Avon, or Aune as many call it. Here the old salmon fishermen's boathouse is a familiar sight so if

you visit it and get that feeling of déjà-vu, it's most probably because this scene has featured on almost every Devon or Westcountry calendar in recent years!

The River Avon is probably Devonshire's loveliest river (and there is plenty of competition). It starts high on Dartmoor at a wet point in the southern wilderness and tumbles ever downwards. Temporarily it is balked by the Avon Dam which supplies the South Hams. In drought years when it is only partially filled, armies of people venture up to it to see what isn't there! The stretch between Avon Dam and Shipley Bridge is extremely popular (see *Ten Family Walks on Dartmoor*) because of its great beauty and public accessibility.

South Brent, with its quaint toll house has that happy distinction of being on the edge of both Dartmoor and the South Hams, a feature no doubt greatly appreciated by its residents. Dartmoor's greatest writer, William Crossing, chose to live there.

The Avon travels on between steep hills in a deep trench-like valley where there are woodland walks with public access. Villages like Diptford and Loddiswell hug the hillsides leaving the river to run its course alone – save for the track bed of the disused Kingsbridge branch line.

From the recently restored Iron-Age hill fort called 'The Rings' there is a tremendous view of the Avon back towards Dartmoor.

Near Aveton Gifford the river takes on its estuarine appearance, with its tidal road visible and usable at low tide yet submerged and out of vehicular bounds at high water. It is a stunningly lovely river and those who have taken the trouble to explore it will, no doubt, endorse this statement.

Bigbury on Sea and the celebrated Burgh Island lie beyond the Avon's sandy mouth. The two are linked by a sandy causeway at low tide and a swirling stretch of water at high tide. At such times the local 'sea monster' plies between the

mainland and the island. There is no public right of way to the top of the island but there is no objection to visitors making their way to the top. But take care as there have been a few deaths, through accident, on the island in recent years.

The huer's hut on top of the island is an excellent vantage point from where virtually the whole sweep of Bigbury Bay can be seen. A huer was a person who kept watch for shoals of fish, usually pilchards, and who called out to fishermen to prepare to cast their nets. It must have been quite a sight to see the sea to the west of the island shining silver in the morning sunshine with millions of these fish.

The pub on the island is appropriately called the Pilchard Inn but if you visit, particularly in August, keep a wary eye open for the ghost of Tom Crocker, a smuggler who was shot dead here.

The Burgh Island Hotel is unusual, something a little out of the ordinary, for if you visit it you will step back in time to the 1930s as the furnishings are from the art deco period. Music of the 1930s and dances are held so if you have a desire to become a 'flapper' this is the place. Agatha Christie spent some time here, enough to write two books, *Evil Under the Sun* and *And then there was None*, the only two titles of hers which rhyme. This was not intentional as the latter was originally called *Ten Little Niggers*.

The island has entertained many famous visitors and was featured in *Holocaust 2000* which starred Kirk Douglas. He 'ran for his life' here to avoid the incoming

tide from both sides. From the 'swinging 60s', the Dave Clark Five ended their film *Catch us if you Can* at this hotel.

The small settlement of Bigbury on Sea is relatively new. In Victorian times it was an open space but by 1910 speculative builders had lined rows of timber chalet style houses in neat rows on the hillside. Many were bought by Plymouth doctors as second homes. They were partly financed as lets to recuperating invalids who seemed to recover more speedily in the bracing Bigbury air.

Challaborough is predominantly a summer holiday camp site, mainly of caravans sited in a valley running down to the coast. Many regard it as a blot on the landscape but it is one which is well concealed and can only be seen from a limited number of places. It provides a perfect centre from which to explore the South Hams. It has grown apace in recent years but seems to have attracted some careless visitors; until quite recently a tiny, almost unnoticeable, bridge near the sea front had a sign on it warning people to take care as, to date, 21 people had fallen in the stream!

The cliffs to the mouth of the Erme are spectacular and the walk along the top of them is not for the faint-hearted, particularly if there is a keen wind wafting from the land side.

Mothecombe is at the mouth of the Erme, a favoured beach spot on those days of the week when its beach is open to the public.

All the lands bordering the Erme Estuary have been under one ownership for more than a century. This has proved an effective form of conservation. If you belong to a school or an interested group, you may get permission to walk this estuary by writing to the estate office at Mothecombe.

Modbury, some say, is a smaller version of Totnes. There are similarities – Totnes has a steep main street ... Modbury's is even steeper. Totnes has a church which can be seen from miles around whilst that of St George in Modbury is a 135 foot high landmark for a great area of surrounding countryside. Some folk say that whilst Totnes had the genius of Charles Babbage, Modbury produced Thomas Savery. He was an inventor, a clockmaker and an engineer who was born in 1650 and who, with Thomas Newcomen, did much to keep tin mines open with his pumps when previously they would have flooded. One of his claims to fame was

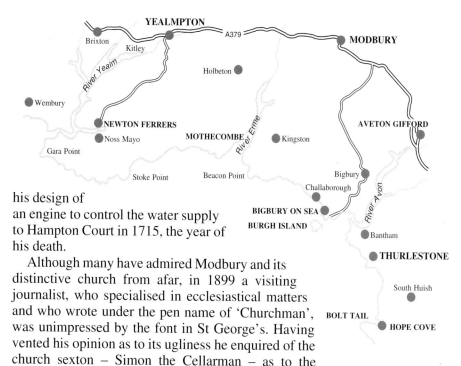

his design of
an engine to control the water supply
to Hampton Court in 1715, the year of
his death.

Although many have admired Modbury and its
distinctive church from afar, in 1899 a visiting
journalist, who specialised in ecclesiastical matters
and who wrote under the pen name of 'Churchman',
was unimpressed by the font in St George's. Having
vented his opinion as to its ugliness he enquired of the
church sexton – Simon the Cellarman – as to the
whereabouts of its more attractive predecessor, which had been removed some
forty years earlier. The journalist was perturbed to discover that it was now in a
neighbouring farmyard where it served as a trough. As the Sexton had local
knowledge of the font, did this also make him the 'font' of local knowledge?

Following a civil war battle near the town, the triumphant cavalry men of the
Parliamentarian force used the church as a stable for all its tired horses. The mother
of Sir Walter Raleigh is buried in the churchyard.

Modbury reached its peak of population in 1821 when it rose to the almighty
figure of 2,194. Today it is proportionately much less and it has changed its
function and character quite drastically. At the time of its peak, almost half the
population were employed in the wool trade. Modbury even sent two members up
to Parliament.

Alas the Industrial Revolution saw a shift in this industry to Yorkshire and thus
the fullers, tuckers, spinners, weavers, dyers and combers lost their livelihoods.
There were other factors which contributed to the decline of the town's prosperity.
For years it served a thriving farming community but the number of agricultural
workers dwindled and those who looked to this for their livelihood suffered.

In the mid nineteenth century when the railways spread throughout the south
west, Modbury found itself stranded well away from the nearest line. However,
later it was planned to bring the railway through from Yealmpton on to Kingsbridge
with the possibility of a branch line going down to Bigbury on Sea. Fortunately

this never happened.

The River Erme rises high up on the boggy morasses of Southern Dartmoor. Like its neighbour, the Avon, it tumbles off its elevated watershed to pass through miles of lonely moorland landscape. It is country which is ideal for exploring on foot, perhaps with the help of books like *Ten Family Walks on Dartmoor* or *Diary of a Dartmoor Walker*.

The Erme plunges down to Ivybridge so its waters have been used to drive waterwheels for a number of mills in the town, most notably Stowford Paper Mill, which has proved to be a major source of employment in the immediate area.

But Ivybridge today is an example of mushroom growth. The green slopes above the town have been invaded by extensive housing estates. Ivybridge is in commuter land, mainly feeding the Plympton and Plymouth area by the A38, the all important speedy 'conveyor belt' which carries the mass morning exodus to its workplace. Until 1973 Ivybridge's long and winding main street played host to all the traffic travelling through it but the building of a new by-pass has proved to be its salvation. The town is believed, in relation to its original size, to be proportionately the fastest growing town in Britain. Set with moors behind, rolling fields below and a great coastline on its near horizon, it's almost the perfect retreat for a committed commuter. The South Dartmoor Leisure Centre is one of several excellent amenities in the town whilst the Tourist Information Centre also shows that Ivybridge is a good base from which to explore this area.

Ermington, a village with about a thousand residents, as its name suggests, is close to the River Erme to the south of Ivybridge. It has a church, dedicated to St Peter, whose spire has been given various titles like the 'Leaning Tower of the South Hams'. It is certainly very bent although how bent it appears depends largely upon from where it is viewed. Legend has it that its crookedness is attributable to the fact that when a certain beautiful young lady, called Miss Bulteel, got married, the spire was so smitten with her lovely looks, it bowed to her in honour. Alas it could not straighten itself and thus remains bent.

Years later repair work was done on the spire after it had been struck by lightning and an opportunity arose to straighten it. However the locals had grown accustomed to it and wished for it to remain leaning. A pub in the village has adopted it for its name so obviously Ermingtonians are that way inclined!

Another legend says that the Devil was so angry that a church was built here that he tried to blow it away but only succeeded in bending the spire.

The River Erme heads on ever southwards twisting through fields and woods before it reaches its gorgeous and protected estuary. Its waters mingle with the sea at Mothecombe where the film *International Velvet* was partly made (see *Made in Devon*). Here Tatum O'Neal rode her horse for the opening and closing sequences of the film.

Walking is the only real way to see the next stretch of coastline from the mouth of the Erme on towards the Yealm, the western limit of our South Hams. Anyone who has survived the walk along the cliffs leading to Erme Mouth will find the next section easy by comparison. This coastline is best walked in the morning when the sun illuminates the entire scene. The unusual St Anchorite's Rock (it is said Anchorite was a miserable old hermit) looks impressive from a distance, yet less so when beside it. An old carriageway provides the perfect pathway on which to trek westwards. It was built for Lord Revelstoke (Edward Baring) in the second half of the nineteenth century. His home was Membland Hall which had a fortune spent on it but to no avail as it was demolished in 1928. In its time it entertained some distinguished visitors, including the Prince of Wales (later Edward VII) and the Tsar of Russia.

The coast path follows the carriageway onward and beyond to the beautiful ruined early fourteenth century cruciform church of St Peter at Stoke which was abandoned in the 1870s. It appears to have its own Co-op caravan park beside it. The walking beyond it is some of the easiest but most enjoyable in Devon. Eventually the carriage-  way leads to our western boundary of the South Hams as it reaches the mouth of the Yealm.

This inlet leads to the twin opposing villages of Noss Mayo and Newton Ferrers. The latter has been ricknamed 'Poor Man's Salcombe' but it has its own identity and is a beautiful spot as well as being a real sun trap. Strangely, guide books seem shy to mention these villages and they get but a brief mention or nothing at all. Perhaps someone with influence has decided to keep this little bit of Devon a secret to stop the masses from spoiling it. Fortunately Newton and Noss are on the road to nowhere so hopefully they will retain their relaxed atmospheres.

Newton Ferrers is perched on a spur between its own creek and the Yealm Estuary. Yealmpton is less than a mile above its tidal limit, an elongated village along the A379. The distinctive church was acclaimed by the late Poet Laureate, Sir John Betjeman, as the most amazing Victorian church in Devon.

I wonder how Sir John, as a man of words, rated another local creation – the rhymes of Old Mother Hubbard. These were written at a large house, 'Kitley', by Sarah Catherine Martin in 1805. Her sister had married into the local gentry – Squire Bastard – and Sarah is believed to have based her rhymes on the housekeeper. The rhyme alludes to a situation which was common across the whole country, among ordinary folk, where food shortages were worse than usual

as a result of the Napoleonic Wars. Sarah had an admirer – Prince William Henry (later to become William IV), the third son of George III. She received many visits from him but circumstances were against their relationship developing into marriage and she died a spinster some four years before he became King. A curious-looking building on the main  road is Mother Hubbard's Cottage. Hopefully the cupboard isn't bare as this is a restaurant now!

A short and pleasant walk from the centre of the village is Kitley Caves, a limestone subterranean world which is open to the public. It's not quite in the same league as the caves at Cheddar, Wookey Hole or Kent's Cavern at Torquay, but it has its own charm, not least its pleasant surroundings.

The Kitley estate borders the estuary and in the past local people wishing to swim here could apply for a bathing pass. There were eight conditions to be fulfilled. These included: bathing was only permitted an hour each side of high tide; bathing drawers or bathing dress had to be worn; no shouting, undue noise or bad language was allowed. Therefore it will be appreciated just how much vocal restraint there must have been when jumping off Kitley Quay into the ice cold waters of the estuary early in the season!

The Kitley estate also once had a small quarry which was unique in Britain, the only one to produce green marble. The staircase in London's Natural History Museum is made from this stone.

Yealmpton was once the terminus of a branch line which ran out from Plymouth. On weekdays six trains a day operated whilst on a Saturday there was

an extra late night train put on for people to go out on the town in Plymouth. It was opened on 15 January 1898 amidst great celebrations, with all the dignitaries of the district present, and survived until 29 February 1960.

In our wanderings though this book we have had but a brief glimpse of an area which is worth exploring if you really want to get away from it all. There are villages like Kingston, Ugborough, Cornworthy, Sherford, South Pool, Loddiswell, Blackawton, Holbeton, East Allington which have hardly had a mention but which are all beautiful in their own way.

There are endless miles of unfrequented green lanes to be explored on foot, stretches of magnificent coastline and hidden valleys and estuaries – but I musn't do too hard a sell as that might spark a visitor invasion! Perhaps if you buy Brian Carter's book *Walks in the South Hams* and follow in his footsteps you will begin to see what we mean when we say this is probably the most beautiful part of Glorious Devon!